Wes's enthusiasm is infectious, his efficiency in teaching enormously productive, and his service as a role model for what an ambitious student can achieve priceless. I count on him to help make dreams come true for my brightest academic stars.

— SCOTT COWAN, TUTOR, FOUNDER OF SF LEARNS

Wes *gets* the brightest students in a way that makes them feel met, and challenged. Wes has helped me see that these kids have special needs. I can think of no better a teacher and a mentor.

— JUSTIN SIGARS, CHIEF INSTRUCTOR, BODSAT PREP

Simply put, there is no better private teacher of mathematics and test preparation for students of exceptional ability in the entire San Francisco Bay Area than Wes Carroll.

— CHRIS BORLAND, OWNER, BORLAND EDUCATIONAL

Wes Carroll has a laser-sharp focus, a quick wit, and connects directly with what a student needs. If you want to further increase your understanding and scores while you decrease your stress, work with Wes.

— BEN BERNSTEIN PHD, AUTHOR OF TEST SUCCESS! HOW TO BE CALM, CONFIDENT AND FOCUSED ON ANY TEST

Wes Carroll's streamlined guide for high achievers delivers bite-sized tools that high schoolers can use to optimize their learning and grades. Ambitious students take note—you'll want to read this book from cover to cover. Probably more than once.

— DAVID MONTESANO, ADMISSION STRATEGIST, COLLEGE MATCH US

There is no better teacher for students of exceptional ability.

— TED DORSEY, FOUNDER, TUTOR TED, INC.

HOW TO BE A BRIGHTER STUDENT

The Craft of Developing Your Brilliance

WES CARROLL

Copyright © 2018 by Wes Carroll

All rights reserved.

No part of this book may be reproduced in any form or by any electronic or mechanical means, including information storage and retrieval systems, without written permission from the author, except for the use of brief quotations in a book review or blog.

❦ Created with Vellum

*For my wife Audrey and my children Mina and Milo;
for my fellow tutors and teachers;
and for my students: past, present, and future.*

CONTENTS

Introduction	ix
1. What is a "bright student"?	1
2. Clean pages don't count	5
3. 10,000 hours?	7
4. Do the steps	11
5. Harnessing your mindset	13
6. Working memory	17
7. Verbatim memory	23
8. Cut when you're sharp	31
9. Stress: a primer	35
10. Training "future you"	43
11. Repeated challenge	47
12. Interlude: How to "win"	53
13. Bite-sized chunks	57
14. Trust yourself, trust the process	61
15. Improve the question	67
16. Struggle with the early material	73
17. Work like an expert	77
18. Steering the supertanker	83
19. DARE: Devise, adjust, repeat, execute	89
20. Be your own pilot	93
Epilogue	105
Afterword	107
Acknowledgments	109
About the Author	111

INTRODUCTION

Through this short book I'll give you a few ideas that have helped me and hundreds of my students. I think of it as an owner's manual for the brilliant mind. I hope it will help you create meaningful change in yourself.

I'm a math guy, so some of this is math advice. But I'm also a mentor and coach, so some of this is life advice. But mostly it's both. So if you have a hard time telling the two apart, don't worry. That's on purpose.

1

WHAT IS A "BRIGHT STUDENT"?

YOU'RE A BRIGHT STUDENT IF YOU LEARN EASILY.

It sometimes seems like there's more to it than that, but that's really the whole ballgame. Everything else we think about bright students—good at school, hard-working, effective in later life and career—all flow from *learning easily*.

YOU CAN IMPROVE HOW BRIGHT YOU ARE.

Most of us also think of "brightness" as an inborn trait: you either have it or you don't. But it doesn't actually work like that. Being bright is largely about your *perspectives* and *habits*, and less about your *inborn qualities* than you might think.

In other words, it's more what you *see* and *understand* and *do* than who you *are*. And since you can change what you see and understand and do, *you can improve how bright you are*.

AN EXAMPLE

I'm reminded of a student I had a few years ago. She was inquisitive, engaged, and whip-smart. But she was also getting a B- in her math class, because she constantly made careless errors. Her advantageous mental ability was no match for her disadvantageous habits of carelessness, and so she wasn't learning as easily as she should have been. Her habits—what she *did*—kept her from being as bright as she could be.

She also had a few false perspectives. For example, although she knew that knowing how to solve problems was important, she incorrectly believed that the act of solving particular problems was beside the point. And although she knew that the material in her current class was important, she incorrectly believed that the previous year's material (which the current class built on) should be de-emphasized or even forgotten now that that class was over. She didn't *see* the class correctly.

Finally, she believed that drill work was only needed in the beginning of the learning process. Once you understood the main principles, the work was no longer necessary. What she later came to *understand* was that through the right kinds of drill work, you can learn to solve certain kinds of problems routinely and without much effort.

It only took a week to get her grade up to an A, and it stayed there for the rest of the school year. More importantly, she now has a permanently better mental toolkit for academic success. She *does* better work, she *sees* what she's doing more clearly, and she better *understands* her own mind. In other words, she's brighter.

She didn't need more smarts. Smarts she had in spades.

What she needed was the right perspective and the right habits.

SUMMARY

You don't need more smarts. You need better perspectives and habits.

2

CLEAN PAGES DON'T COUNT

A smart man makes a mistake, learns from it, and never makes that mistake again. But a wise man finds a smart man and learns from him how to avoid the mistake altogether.

— ROY H. WILLIAMS

GO GET A PENCIL, RIGHT NOW

THE ONE RULE of this book is *as you read it, mark it up and write in the margins.* (Note: for electronic books, highlighting and annotation will work just fine instead.)

Doing so will help you answer three key questions:

1. What does this say?
2. What does this mean?
3. Why does this matter to me?

You'll find that this is a good habit to apply to other books you'll read as well.

The general idea here is not to think of a book as a fully-prepared meal that you will eat in order to become less hungry; instead, a book is more like a shopping bag fresh from the grocery store. It contains ingredients that go together, but you still have to do some work to make it into something that will feel good going in, and will become a useful part of you.

I MEAN IT

If you haven't already, get that pencil now.

3

10,000 HOURS?

You don't have to make yourself miserable to be successful. Success isn't about working hard, it's about working smart.

— ANDREW WILKINSON

WHEN IT COMES TO HOMEWORK, MORE IS NOT BETTER

YOU'VE PROBABLY HEARD of Outliers ("The Story of Success"), Malcolm Gladwell's 2008 opus, based in part on research by Anders Ericsson. Even if you haven't read it yourself, it's probably been quoted to you. It's the main source of the idea in popular culture that true mastery requires ten thousand hours of practice, which in turn has been used to justify all manner of craziness, including too much homework.

Let's set the record straight: Gladwell's book is not the source of the craziness *per se*. The craziness happened because somewhere between Ericsson's original research and the reports on Gladwell's book in the popular press, the proper context and conclusions got lost.

Gladwell (or at least those who reported on his book) popularized the idea that across a wide variety of fields, and especially in cognitively demanding ones, true mastery generally requires a minimum of ten thousand hours of a particular kind of practice.

A common misreading of this observation was the notion that since it's the magical 10,000 number that determines successful mastery, one should get in as many hours as one can, as soon as one can. Hence, for example, never-ending homework assignments.

This sounds good, but unfortunately *it isn't what the research actually showed.*

THE RIGHT KIND OF PRACTICE IS SMART

The research showed that *the right kind of practice leads to improvement, and the wrong kind of practice does not.*

This is true no matter how much practice you put in. However you define "mastery," the right kind of practice will get you there fastest. Furthermore, continued correct practice will continue to improve your skills. (The 10,000 hours number comes from the observation that when you are competing with other people, being the best depends on putting in an *enormous* quantity of the right kind of practice, because everyone you are competing with will be doing the same.)

Let's get practical. How do we do this, and what else can we learn here?

The main thing is to stop practicing mindlessly. Believe it or not, practice doesn't actually make perfect, no matter what people say. Instead, practice simply makes *permanent*; only *perfect practice* makes perfect.

So what is perfect practice? It's a situation that challenges your current ability. So strive at every session to work ever so slightly beyond the highest level you can reach. It's demanding, frustrating, and often annoying work. Generally, it can't be done for more than about three hours a day. It is not generally pleasant. But it works.

MAKE YOUR WORK BETTER

So remember: *quality, not quantity* of practice is the most important factor. Even a hundred hours of quality practice will move the needle. On the other hand, though, you could spend your whole life practicing something by rote and never get any better. (Do you hear me, teachers who assign piles of mindless work?)

Your goal shouldn't be to do a ton of work, and your teacher's goal shouldn't be to pile it on. Instead, the goal should be to *make your work better*. The better your work, the less of it you will need, and the faster you will progress. Avoid the kind of inefficient work that doesn't get you closer to mastery.

YOU DON'T NEED MORE SMARTS

Another important lesson here is that although talent matters, it doesn't matter much. Most of life isn't actually a "more talent is better" situation. Rather, it's more like "you must be at least this tall to ride this ride." Some talent is necessary, but beyond that, more is not appreciably better. "A basketball player only has to be tall enough—and the same is true of intelligence. Intelligence has a threshold," says Gladwell.

So, do smarts matter? Yes, but not as much as you think. *You are already smart enough* to be doing what you're attempting. Believe it or not, being smarter wouldn't help you all that much.

In pretty much any area of human endeavor, people have a tremendous capacity to improve their performance, as long as they train in the right way. If you practice something in the right way for a few hundred hours, you will almost certainly see great improvement. And from there, you can keep going and going and going, getting better and better and better. How much you improve is up to you.

SUMMARY

What matters most is how well you practice.

4

DO THE STEPS

The scientist never takes two steps at a time. And neither can you.

— LOREN EISELEY

HOW MASTERS WORK

IF YOU SAW me solving a difficult math puzzle, you'd see me writing things down for no apparent reason. You'd see me multiplying numbers in strange ways. You'd see me drawing pictures that don't seem related to the puzzle. You'd probably think I was half-crazy. There's no obvious pattern to it.

When you watch any master at work, you usually see the master doing only some of the steps, and skipping the rest.

Or do you?

It certainly seems that way. And *because* it seems that way, we all have the idea that getting good at something means skipping most of the steps. So, we try to skip steps. Plus, skipping steps feels good because it feels fast. We like to go fast. Experts go fast.

But that isn't how it really works. Speed isn't mastery. *Experts don't actually skip steps.*

Instead, they've practiced those steps many, many times before. Therefore, they do some of the steps so comfortably, so naturally, that it looks from the outside as though they aren't doing them at all.

So, when trying to copy masters, don't copy what you see them doing. Aim instead to copy all the parts of their process. This will mean paying special attention to the parts that are hard to see. You'll have to slow the process down to an extraordinary degree at first.

AIM ONLY FOR ACCURACY

The real lesson I'm trying to give you here is that you shouldn't aim to skip steps, and you shouldn't try to work more quickly than you can. You should always work deliberately, carefully, accurately. What I've found again and again is that the more carefully you work, the faster you will become in the end. However, if you try to make yourself work more quickly, your work will become shoddy, and you will have to spend even more time checking and correcting.

∼

SUMMARY

Practice for accuracy, so that you will become both accurate and fast. Don't practice for speed; that will make your work both slow and wrong in the end.

5
HARNESSING YOUR MINDSET

Do not be embarrassed by your failures. Learn from them and start again.

— RICHARD BRANSON

INTELLIGENCE, LIKE STRENGTH, IS CHANGEABLE

In 2006, Carol Dweck of Stanford published Mindset ("The new psychology of success / How we can learn to fulfill our potential"). Dr. Dweck's big revelation was that the growth of your intelligence depends in large part on what you think intelligence is.

On one hand, if you think of your intelligence as changeable (like for example your strength), then you will tend to challenge it, and thus increase it. On the other, if you think of your intelligence as a fixed trait (like, for example, your height), then you will tend to avoid challenging it, for fear that you might fail. That is, you'll try to protect it from being "discovered" to be flawed. Then, without the exercise it needs, your intelligence will lose power.

Even better: think of your intelligence in the same way you might think of compound interest. An intelligence that gets even a tiny bit bigger each day can, over years and decades, come to dwarf any stagnant intelligence, no matter how big a head start the stagnant one had at first.

IT'S GOOD TO BE WRONG

If you aim to *prove you're smart* or *prove you're right*, you'll stunt your own mental growth. However, if you set out *to learn*, and accept that part of the process is sometimes looking dumb and sometimes being wrong, then you'll accelerate your mental growth.

Those with the most successful mindsets welcome failure. That's because they know that being wrong is the necessary first step in the process of becoming right. Aim to discover your failures so that you can examine and ultimately correct them. And remember the compound interest analogy: the more you're willing to be wrong and maybe even look a bit foolish, the less frequently you will actually be foolish in the long run.

It's easier said than done, of course, but every step you take in this direction will pay off.

So when you catch yourself not knowing something that you think you ought to know, recognize that uncomfortable feeling...and then keep going. That discomfort can help you improve your habits and knowledge for the better. Just hold on to that feeling for as long as it takes to fill the gap in your knowledge or habits. Then let the feeling go, as you pat yourself on the back for having improved yourself.

Realizing when you're wrong is one of the most empowering realizations you can have. Learning to be excited about (and even grateful for) that feeling it is one of the most empowering habits you can create in yourself.

SUMMARY

Intelligence grows through exercise. The key is to try your best, and when you fail, to examine your failure critically.

WORKING MEMORY

Yesterday is but today's memory, and tomorrow is today's dream.

— KAHLIL GIBRAN

YOU'RE THE NEXT CONTESTANT

IMAGINE that you are the next contestant on a game show for which the top prize is ten million dollars. You will be asked to do complicated calculations, and if you get them all right, you will become fabulously rich.

But there's a catch: you must do all your work on tiny whiteboards, so small that each can hold only a part of the work you must do for each calculation. But wait—it gets worse. The show's producers have several assistants. As you work on one whiteboard, the assistants subtly but significantly change tiny bits of your work on the other whiteboards, copying your handwriting as well as they can.

At first your job seemed to be one of mere calculation, but now you can see that your job is mainly fraud detection.

You must notice the errors introduced by the wily assistants, while you are also busy solving maddeningly difficult problems.

This bizarre scenario is surprisingly analogous to the situation inside your brain every time you work on any multi-stage computation or decision.

Let's back up for a minute and look at this more closely.

TYPES OF MEMORY

When you think of *memory*, you're probably thinking of what psychologists call *long-term memory*. It tells you what you ate for breakfast, as well as how awesome your last birthday party was. Or maybe you're thinking of *procedural memory*, which tells you how to tie your shoes and ride a bike.

But I'd like to tell you about the part called *working memory*. Working memory only tells you what you were thinking about *up to about ten seconds ago*. It's super-short-term memory, and you use it all the time. For example, when you try to multiply numbers in your head, working memory is where you put the intermediate steps. Working memory is also how you remember parts of the last sentence while you're reading this one. It allows you to connect the two.

In a multi-step process, working memory is where you remember which steps to do when. For example, to heat frozen food, first you take the food out of the freezer, then you open the package, then you put it into the microwave, then you press the button. Or, to change lanes, first you check your blind spot, then you hit the turn signal, then you move the steering wheel. At these times, you're keeping mental track of the steps of the procedure. The place where you do that is your working memory.

HOW YOUR MEMORY IS FLAWED

Since you use it so much, you should understand your working memory and its limitations.

Here are some facts about working memory:

1. It holds up to about four or five things at a time (which is part of why phone numbers are hard to memorize)
2. It holds things for only a few seconds, and then its contents get deleted (leaving only the frustrating impression of having remembered something, rather than leaving any hint as to what the thing actually was)
3. Just before losing something, working memory often changes the thing (e.g. making that phone number wrong by one or two digits just as you finish finding a pen or opening the app that would let you get it down)
4. There is no warning or check mechanism alerting you that the contents of working memory have changed
5. There is no way to recover lost working memory
6. Attempting to overfill working memory causes the forgetting mechanism mentioned in point 2 and the changing mechanism mentioned in point 3 to happen *even faster than normal*, and again with no warning or recovery method

This list probably *feels* false. We are used to thinking of our memories as mostly infallible (at least before our 40th birthday or so), and we certainly don't consider the possibility that something that we just committed to memory would change itself seconds later. But it does, leaving us with the certain (but nonetheless incorrect) sense that we know exactly what we were thinking.

GETTING AROUND THESE FLAWS

Once you've played with these facts enough to see that they are true, and overcome your quite reasonable horror, you'll probably next come to a few obvious questions. How have I survived this long with such a defective brain? And how can I stop having problems related to these defects? (Unfortunately, I can't help you with that first question. I sometimes wonder how we made it this far in the first place.)

What I *can* tell you is that the answer to the second question not only exists, but you probably have it in your home: it's paper and a pen or pencil. ***When you write, you avoid the fatal flaw in your memory***.

See, when your sixth grade math teacher traumatized you by constantly taking off points for not showing your work, she really was trying to help you. She wanted you to build the skill of representing the intermediate steps of your thought process on paper, because graphite on paper not only doesn't change what it's saying (unless you change it on purpose), but also doesn't disappear (unless you bought your pencil at a practical joke store). These two properties make pencil and paper a *critically important upgrade* to the normal function of your brain. It's why we practice so many processes on paper in school. It's also why we have grocery lists. In both cases, we need to keep track of something for longer than working memory lasts, but we don't need to commit it to long-term memory for permanent retrieval. Pencil and paper does the job.

HOW EGO GETS IN THE WAY

Ironically, bright students are usually the last in their classes to take advantage of this upgrade. That's because they often think especially quickly, and so their (normal) working memories last through relatively difficult calculations. As a result, they often get caught in a rut: they work problems in their heads, they get the answer quickly (since working memory, for all its flaws, is faster than pencil and paper), they take pride in the speed of their work, and so they decide to continue to work problems in their heads. (Whoops! See Chapter 4, "Do the steps," and Chapter 5, "Harnessing your mindset," to learn why this is a series of mistakes.)

Sadly, they are headed for a crisis. No matter how efficient their brains are, these students will very soon be asked to solve problems that are far too complicated to do without pencil and paper. Meanwhile, their less speedy classmates learn earlier the limitations of holding everything in their heads, and develop the skill of capturing thoughts on paper. Thus the merely competent students begin to outpace those thought to be especially gifted. It's a classic case of *good habits beating raw talent*.

As a result, sooner or later, the "slow" student will be able to do complicated calculations that the "smart" student can't. It's just that one student has learned to smoothly transfer the contents of working memory to a permanent medium, but the other student—supposedly the smart one—just gets frustrated at not being able to hold the whole thing in his or her head for quite long enough. (Which is not actually that smart.)

The fix is simple: make better friends with paper starting immediately, and get over whatever pride is falsely telling you that you don't need it.

Because you really do need it.

SUMMARY

If you want to be right more, write more.

7
VERBATIM MEMORY

I consider that a man's brain originally is like a little empty attic, and you have to stock it with such furniture as you choose.

— SHERLOCK HOLMES (A. C. DOYLE)

A good mnemonic is a joy forever.

— JOHN KEATS (MORE OR LESS)

THINGS HAVE CHANGED

MOST OF THE world's knowledge is available on your phone.

This is new. Half a generation ago, this didn't exist.

It's wonderful, but it also creates a problem. The problem is that today's teachers aren't great at teaching you to be effective in an environment in which facts are so available. Even if they've had excellent training, they just haven't had all that much personal experience with this situation yet.

This is important because some kinds of information

really need to be in your head in order to be valuable. But most kinds do not. And it can be hard to tell the difference.

WHAT TO MEMORIZE

Load up on frameworks and basic facts; research the rest.

Five good rules of thumb are:

1. If timing matters, then **do** memorize it
2. If it's very easy to look up, then **don't** memorize it
3. If you've looked it up three times in the past, then **do** memorize it
4. Before you memorize it, **make sure** it's right
5. If you'll be tested on it, memorize it **early**

Rule #1 really means that you should memorize anything that is usually part of an "intermediate step." So, for example, memorizing times tables is still generally a good idea if you are going to be doing any serious multiplication by hand, since (for example) if you want to calculate 46 times 57, one of the necessary intermediate steps is multiplying the six by the seven. You don't want to have to look that up in the middle of your calculation. (See Chapter 6, "Working memory," if you don't understand why that's critically important.)

Similarly, if you are going to have to organize essays for a history class by chronology, then a necessary intermediate step will be associating events with dates. Here, memorization makes sense.

Notice here that the reason for memorizing is to be able to do other things with the memorized information later. Too often we incorrectly think of memorizing as the goal, and that can lead to being satisfied with getting it 80% right. Instead, keep it in perspective. You are building a base of knowledge, and you are going to build a "tower" of complex knowledge on top of this base later. Getting the base 100% right is worth the extra effort, so that it will support a tower that is both tall and stable.

Another way to say **rule #2** is that if it's easy to ask the question, and you can find an answer quickly, then it's not worth committing to memory.

For example, you can easily find the Value-Added Tax rate in Germany, the length of the longest day of the year at 35 degrees latitude, and the integral from 0 to 1 of sin x. These are not worth memorizing.

On the other hand, you probably can't easily find why the Value-Added Tax exists in Europe but not in the US, how changes in latitude change the length of the longest day, or techniques for proving the validity of trigonometric integrals. So these might be worth digging into.

Rule #3 tells you to use your memory on the things that matter most to you. This makes you a better thinker in the areas of your interest, because having things in your memory allows you to think about them at any time, with none of the delays caused by having to look things up.

Regarding **rule #4**: fact-checking is difficult, but it's especially important for the things you're going to put into your head permanently. So obey this rule. After all, as Abraham Lincoln famously said, "Don't believe most of what you read on the Internet, especially quotes from famous people."

Rule #5 is usually first on people's lists, because they are used to having teachers tell them what to memorize and what not to memorize. But I think it's a good idea to take more responsibility for what you'll choose to memorize. So I put this rule at the end. And I included the unexpected word "early," because memorizing material for a test early means you'll probably have to re-memorize it close to the test. As you'll see below, that means you'll probably retain it for a lot longer: until the final exam, and beyond.

MEMORIZATION IS A SKILL

Memory isn't actually as good as we all think it is. We usually think of memory as a digital camera with more or less infinite capacity: anything we see or hear, we can probably remember pretty well. But that's not how it actually is. It's imperfect. So we need to *learn* how to use it best.

For starters, it's more like a painting than a photograph. That is, *interpretation* is a much bigger piece of the process than we realize. What we remember and how we remember it have a lot to do with how we interpret what we saw or heard. So when we think we remember "what happened" or "what the book said," we usually only really remember what we *perceived* or what we *understood*.

And we don't do even that perfectly. And it fades over time, usually more than we realize. And it can change, often without our realizing it.

Memory is imperfect in a lot of ways. If you expect it to be perfect, which it isn't, then that's a problem. But if you accept it for what it is, you can use its strengths without getting hurt by its weaknesses. Learn how it works best, so you can get the best out of it.

Start by thinking about what human memory was developed for in the first place.

- We use language, so we remember *words*.
- We are social creatures, so we remember *stories*.
- We move through a changing environment, so we remember *where we've been*, and *what was there*.
- Our most recent experiences and our repeated experiences are usually the most relevant. So mostly *we forget what isn't recent or repeated*.

These observations help us to understand our limited memories.

HOW TO MEMORIZE: THE ANCIENT EDITION

Now, let's take advantage of the classic wisdom. Look up the **method of loci**, also known as a *mind palace* or *memory palace*. This technique is great for improving your direct retrieval of *ordered* lists, e.g. the periodic table of elements. Since this method is very easy to look up, I'm not even going to explain it. All you really need is its name, and you'll find all the resources you could want (and more).

Also, you should be aware of the incredible effectiveness of **flash cards**. Flash cards are great for strengthening your retrieval of *unordered* lists, e.g. foreign-language vocabulary.

HOW TO MEMORIZE: THE MODERN EDITION

There are many computer and smartphone apps that do the work of flash cards without the actual cards. As of this writing, *Quizlet* is a popular example. Many, including Quizlet, give you the ability to easily access sets of cards made by others, allowing you to get you started almost instantly. (Note: as you'll see in Chapter 16, "Struggle with the early material," you might be better off making your cards yourself, even though it takes more work at first.)

Modern research has also supercharged flash cards by giving us a refined technique called **spaced repetition**. This technique is based on the research that shows that the best way to memorize something permanently is to be quizzed on it just as you are about to forget it. If you do this consistently, then the things that you are memorizing will "stick" for longer and longer every time you quiz yourself. The only catch is that you have to get the timing right.

There are lots of ways to accomplish this, but the easiest is to use an application like *Anki* that works out the timing for you, and gives you the right quiz at just the right time.

Four other ideas I'll mention here are *internal context*, *external context*, *chunking*, and *mnemonics*.

If I mention a stranger's name to you, it's just a name. But if I mention the name of your best friend, you instantly remember all kinds of details about who they are, what they like, when you last saw them, and so forth. That's an example of **internal context** in action. It's the idea that when you are very familiar with something, remembering it also causes you to remember a ton of associated context, which makes the memory even more useful.

The important idea here is that it works in both directions. In other words, thinking about the associated context helps you to remember the idea itself. Make this work for you: when you're having trouble remembering something important, it helps to think about all the things that it connects to.

Good homework makes you create these associations automatically, by asking you questions that make you consider the pieces of the subject in relation to each other.

If the information in a class feels "jumbled" or "disconnected," you probably need more internal context and connections. Start by thinking about how individual pieces of the material connect to other pieces.

When you have enough of these associations within a subject that you're studying, the whole subject will start to feel "obvious," as though there is no other way the pieces could fit together. The pieces will be very well-connected in your mind. If any of the pieces get lost or try to change, you'll notice the "hole" or "mistake" in your knowledge, and you'll correct it easily—even automatically.

External context, also called state-based learning, is the idea that it's easier to remember things when you're in the physical environment where you learned them in the first place. It even works with imaginary environments, which is part of how the method of loci works.

Chunking is the practice of grouping items together to make them easier to remember. For example, the ten letters *DADECDEBCB* would be hard to memorize, but the four "words" DA, DEC, DEB, and CB would be easier. By grouping them into chunks, we've made them easier to memorize.

Mnemonics are acronyms, songs, or other cues that help you remember things, especially lists. For example, the silly sentence "My very educated mother just served us nachos" is much easier to remember than the names of the eight planets (in order from closest to farthest from the sun). But the eight words of the sentence starts with the same eight letters as the names of the planets: Mercury, Venus, Earth, Mars, Jupiter, Saturn, Uranus, Neptune. So the silly sentence is a great way to remember the names of the planets.

Of course, the techniques can be combined. For example, mnemonics are often chunked together.

Here are some examples of common memory aids:

- "HONC 1234" reminds chemistry students the number of bonds linking hydrogen, oxygen, nitrogen, and carbon atoms, respectively.
- "Five tomato" (five-two-eight-oh) is the number of feet in a mile.
- "All students take calculus" helps precalculus students remember the quadrants in which the sine, tangent, and cosine functions have positive (rather than negative) values.
- "Camels ordinarily sit down carefully; perhaps their joints creak." Now you know the first letters

of the names of the periods of the Paleozoic and Mesozoic Eras.

And of course, you'll develop many of your own. Perhaps you already have.

∼

SUMMARY

Having the world's knowledge in your phone doesn't mean you don't need to memorize. It just means that what *you need to memorize is different from what previous generations had to memorize.*

Understand how you use what you've memorized, so that you can make better choices about what to memorize.

Then, understand what is easy for your brain, you can get it to remember what you need it to.

8

CUT WHEN YOU'RE SHARP

If everything were perfect, you would never learn and you would never grow.

— BEYONCE KNOWLES

TOOLS ARE RELIABLE

A GOOD TOOL—a machine, a computer, a vehicle—does its job reliably: the same way every time, as many times as you need it done.

We like to think of our bodies and minds as tools in this same way. Ask them to get something done for us, and we expect them to do the thing, just like they did many times in the past.

...BUT YOU ARE NOT

But of course that isn't how it works. We can be tired or energetic, enthusiastic or grumpy, eager or afraid, curious or withdrawn, hungry or sated, healthy or under the weather; the list of possibilities goes on and on. We don't work like tools; our minds and bodies are not machines; *we are not reliably uniform* in our outputs.

In fact, you're probably already aware that what you can get done on a great day is probably a hundred times what you can get done when you're sick in bed all day. The unexpected and interesting thing is that it's doesn't take the drama of a "great day" or "sick in bed" to affect your effectiveness enormously. Our output is even more variable than we realize.

There are a couple of useful insights to be gained from this observation.

LEARN YOUR CYCLES, AND USE THEM

Brains don't work optimally at all times. But you *can* predict when and how to get your best work out of your brain. That's because are mostly *predictable*, even if they aren't totally reliable.

So first, *understand the things that most affect you* so that you can prevent the worst effects (and bolster the best ones). The biggest items on this list are usually sleep quantity and sleep quality: most people would be a lot more effective if they got more and better sleep. Another biggie is exercise: if you run cross-country, for example, you have a huge academic edge over a couch potato. Diet also plays a role: properly balancing proteins, fats, and carbohydrates helps, as does minding glycemic index, and intake of caffeine, and the like.

Second is that as you become more aware of your cycles, you can work with them instead of against them. For example, let's say you discover that you do your best work in the morning, and let's say you have the option to take the AP version of a class. Then whether the class meets in the morning should factor in to your decision.

The better your awareness, the more benefit you'll get. I

recommend journaling as a good way of increasing your awareness of your own cycles.

Third, learn to recognize the feeling of "working against yourself." For example, if you're trying to do highly focused work while you're sleepy, it's going to feel weird, and you aren't going to make as much progress as you might otherwise expect. In that case, see the situation for what it is, and *go easy on yourself*. It seems sometimes that the natural reaction for most people in that situation is to get upset that they aren't able to perform at their best whenever they want to. But if you know when you do your best kinds of work, you won't have this expectation or problem. It all starts with learning your unique cycles, and how to best use them to your advantage.

RECOGNIZE YOUR MODES, AND USE THEM TOO

Finally, as you get farther into this, you'll discover that it isn't just a question of "how good you are" at any given moment, but rather how good you are *for a particular purpose*. We not only ebb and flow in our overall focus and productivity from moment to moment and from day to day and from season to season, but we also experience "modes" in which we are especially well-suited to certain kinds of activities, but not others. For example, many successful people have found that they are particularly creative or particularly focused at certain times of day. Such successful people have crafted their daily schedules to take advantage of these strengths. Others have found that a daily nap at a particular time of day is especially restorative.

As I mentioned before, journaling really helps you to become aware of your own modes and preferences.

This is like identifying as a "morning person" or "night person," but takes it a step beyond simply knowing when you are at your most energetic. If you categorize your work (and, for that matter, your play) into many types, you will likely find that you become more efficient and effective simply by putting the right kind of activity into the right place in your daily schedule.

And it isn't limited to your *daily* schedule, either.

∽

SUMMARY

Your mind is like a knife that is sometimes sharp... but sometimes not so much. Aim to bolster your average through better self-care, and learn to recognize your peaks and valleys through better self-knowledge. Then you can more easily and reliably "cut when you're sharp."

9

STRESS: A PRIMER

In times of stress, the best thing we can do for each other is to listen with our ears and our hearts, and to be assured that our questions are just as important as our answers.

— FRED ROGERS

WHAT IS STRESS TO YOU?

AS YOU KNOW, stress is an unavoidable part of student culture. Understand how it's affecting you, so that you can change your relationship to stress and its effects.

STRESS IS COMPLICATED

Defining stress is surprisingly difficult. Some say stress is a certain pattern of thoughts. Some say it's a physical process or reaction. Some say it's a kind of misalignment or disconnection between various parts of your mind or body or even spirit.

When *I* talk about stress, I'm talking about what the

psychologists call *arousal:* it means "how amped up your nervous system is at the moment."

I think of it mostly as a *physical process* that starts because of something in your *environment* or in your *mind*.

I have seen its effects in my students and in myself for many years. Here are a few tools that I hope will improve your relationship with stress.

WHAT STRESS FEELS LIKE

Common signs of mild stress include:

- Increased heart rate
- Change in posture
- Breathing more quickly and shallowly

As stress gets more severe, the reactions become more like these:

- Feeling of butterflies in the stomach
- Sweaty palms
- Overwhelming emotions
- Headache or other physical pain

Sometimes the best way to gauge your stress level is to pay attention to your body, and whether it is exhibiting any of these symptoms.

Some stress is okay and can even be helpful. But too much is not okay.

TOO MUCH IS A PROBLEM

There are three main ways in which too much stress can cause trouble.

1. It reduces your ability to do certain kinds of mental work
2. It can become a habit: feeling some stress today can make you feel more stress tomorrow
3. Too much of it over too long a time can cause health problems

TOO LITTLE CAN BE A PROBLEM, TOO

The opposite of stress isn't calm, it's *boredom*. You might want that when it's time to go to bed, but you don't want it when you are trying to deliver a peak performance. In that case, you want to be energized but not jittery, excited but not anxious, focused but a little "loose."

IT CHANGES YOUR ABILITIES

Here's a graph showing how stress can make you more or less capable:

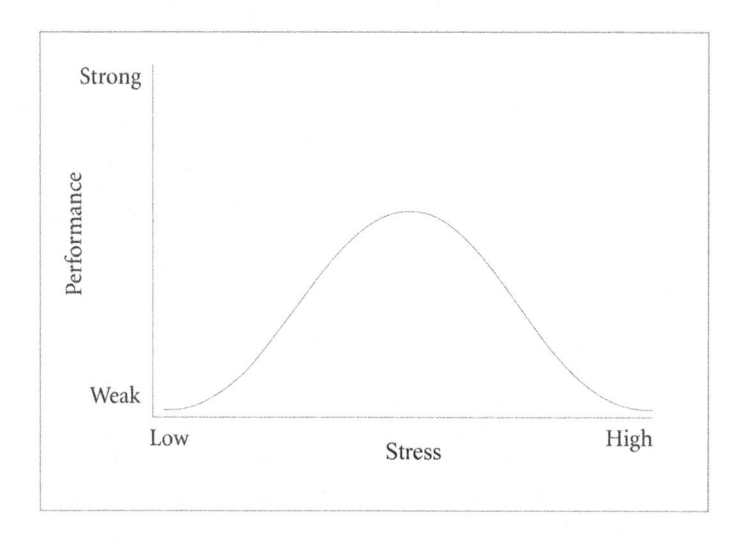

You can see that when you want to perform at your best, you need some stress. A medium amount is best.

If this doesn't match up with your experience, it could be because you spend most of your time on the right-hand side of the curve, too stressed too often. This kind of long-term overstress can be surprisingly difficult to notice, because when you experience stress over a long period of time, you lose the ability to perceive it. It becomes a "new normal." If this describes you, you need tools for reducing your stress. Skip to the end of this chapter.

Another reason why this graph could feel wrong is that you might spend too much of your time on the wrong kind of thinking.

That's because the above graph is based on a certain kind of challenging thinking and tasks. However, if you mostly spend time and energy on simple tasks, then a different graph will be more helpful to you:

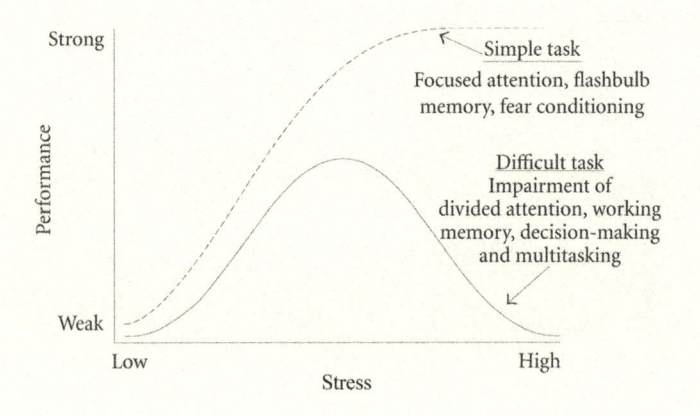

Graph: Performance (Weak to Strong) vs. Stress (Low to High). Simple task curve: rises and plateaus at Strong — Focused attention, flashbulb memory, fear conditioning. Difficult task curve: inverted U peaking at medium stress — Impairment of divided attention, working memory, decision-making and multitasking.

Here you can see that the effect stress has on you depends on which kind of mental task you're doing. Simple tasks and simple thoughts are less susceptible to the negative effects of overstress.

So if you think that stress doesn't hurt your ability to function, it could be because you aren't challenging yourself with difficult mental tasks.

IT'S NOT ALL BAD

Usually people think of stress as a bad thing. But the previous graphs suggest otherwise. Why is there a difference between what we believe, and what the data shows?

Maybe it's because we're thinking about stress in the wrong way.

Go back to the list of symptoms in "What stress feels like." Of course, you've experienced some of these symptoms during a big test or a big match. But look again: you've also experienced them when you're about to go on a roller coaster, or trying something new, or meeting someone new (especially if you think that that person is cute).

My point is that you feel stress at lots of times, some bad, and some good.

Think carefully about what causes symptoms of stress in your life. The causes probably aren't actually all bad. But they are probably all *difficult*. In fact, a good synonym for "stressful" is "challenging."

Some stress is actually good. The trick is to really get to know what stress feels like. Once you are familiar with the feeling of the "right amount" of stress, and also with the feeling of too much stress, you'll be able to do a better job of adjusting your stress level whenever you need to. You'll be able to keep it in the right zone for peak performance, for comfort, and for good health.

A PATTERN WORTH FIXING

Sometimes, when you are feeling just the right amount of stress, you misinterpret that stress as a bad feeling, and start worrying that "something must be wrong." This increases your stress, which in turn increases your worry, and before you know it, bam, you're out of the sweet spot.

If you recognize this pattern in yourself, try to stop thinking of stress as a part of you. Instead think of stress as something that is happening *to* you and your body. Your body feels these reactions for lots of reasons, some good and some bad, and sometimes it even happens for no apparent reason at all. When you feel stress, notice it, and ask yourself why you feel it.

Learn to interpret the feeling of "just enough" stress as a good feeling: *it's what your body feels like when you are primed for a peak performance.*

If something bad is actually happening, thank your body for the surge of adrenaline and get on with dealing with the situation. Otherwise, use the following list to lower the stress level in your body.

HOW TO CHANGE YOUR STRESS LEVEL

This list is just a start:

- Take one deep breath
- Look out the window for a moment
- Walk around for a few minutes
- "Watch yourself from the outside" for a moment
- Have a drink of water
- Have a snack, especially a healthy one like fruit or nuts
- Explore tactile soothing, i.e., get a fidget tool

- Think about what the situation will be like five minutes from now
- Journal about your stress
- Get some exercise
- Change your environment (e.g. clean your desk)
- Read a book on stress reduction
- See a professional

SUMMARY

Proper stress is actually good. Only overstress (or understress) is bad. Learn to recognize the difference. Then get to work changing your own stress levels, so that you can better stay in the "sweet spot."

EXPERT LEVEL

Check out Test Success! by Ben Bernstein, and The Upside Of Stress by Kelly McGonigal.

10

TRAINING "FUTURE YOU"

I am not a product of my circumstances. I am a product of my decisions.

— STEPHEN COVEY

YOU ARE THE PRODUCT OF DECISIONS

FOR THE MOST PART, you are the product of decisions you made in your past. For example: you went to the gym and so you are stronger. You ate a donut and so you are heavier (or perhaps merely more energetic). You practiced your Spanish so now you are closer to fluent. And so on.

In the same way, you will become the product of the decisions you are making *now*. You are going to the gym, or not. You are eating a donut, or not. You are practicing your Spanish, or not. And therefore future you will be different from current-you in some predictable ways.

YOU ARE CREATING "FUTURE YOU" ALL THE TIME

A key error people usually make when deciding on what to do with their time is to assume that they themselves will benefit from or be hurt by their decisions. But that is not quite true. It would be more accurate to say that your decisions now affect someone else, namely "future you." "Current you" will not change much because of your current actions, and even if you do experience change, that change may well be detrimental. For example, going to the gym doesn't make current you strong; it merely makes current you sore and sweaty. Ah, but future you might get enormous benefits. The best part, of course, is that *soon you will become future you*. Whether good or bad, whatever qualities you build into future you will become yours, because future you is the person you will become, whether you want to or not.

The toughest part is that the human mind is wired to drastically overweight any effects on your present, and to underweight the effects on your future. In other words, we care deeply about current us, and we really don't care much about future us. That bias is built into us all. It's a flaw in our collective mental software, and by and large we aren't even aware of this flaw.

So, if you think about planning for *your own* future, you're likely to undershoot the mark. You can avoid that mistake with a simple tiny change in perspective.

FUTURE YOU IS SOMEONE ELSE

The "life hack" that will help you get better future mileage out of your decisions is: *think of future you as a separate person.*

That's helpful because even though we are not wired to properly make decisions about our own future, we *are* properly wired to make good decisions about *other people*.

This is why, for example, most people trying to do their homework find "it will make me feel good to have it done" to be a poor motivator. However, those same people are able to train hard for their sports teammates.

Think of your future self as a separate person — a teammate, if you will. Future you needs all the help you can give him or her, and in return, he or she will give you a better life later on.

∽

SUMMARY

You can make better decisions by thinking of your future self as a separate person.

EXPERT LEVEL

Once you get used to doing this, here are some "expert-level" questions you might consider:

1. *How are future me's preferences like mine, and how are they different?*
2. *How much control over those preferences can I express through my actions and decisions today?*
3. *How can I take advantage of the answers to these questions?*

One other piece of advice: when work that you've done in the past helps you now, take a moment to thank past you. That satisfaction can be a good motivator for you to help future you even more.

11

REPEATED CHALLENGE

The mechanic who would perfect his work must first sharpen his tools.

— CONFUCIUS

Now, let's shift our focus from the *creation* of future you to the *tools* we will give to him or her.

I'd like to focus specifically on the theme of *repeated challenge*, since that's what the future version of you is going to be grappling with. From our point of view, we might even say that that is the point of future you: he or she is going to handle challenges like your current challenges, *only better*.

So let's see how "better handling" of repeated challenges actually works.

HOW MOST OF US THINK ABOUT REPEATED CHALLENGE

Most of us believe, incorrectly but stubbornly, that after we've overcome a challenge once, we will automatically overcome all future similar-looking challenges, as illustrated by this story:

> Henry has done most of his homework for a class, but the last question is of a type he doesn't think he has seen before. He tries a few methods suggested by the current chapter, but nothing seems to work. He feels a little anxious, but he decides to give it a break for dinner. After dinner, he goes back to your desk, and the solution hits him! He finishes the question and finishes his homework, and closes his notebook triumphantly.
>
> Next week, he gets stuck again while working on his homework. Again it's a type of problem he doesn't think he has seen before, just like last week. And he figures that he'll probably solve it quickly and easily, just because he solved it quickly and easily last time.

Note the mistake in the story Henry tells himself: it wasn't quick and easy the first time, and it won't be quick and easy the second time either. But if we are very careful to keep track of the details of how we solved the problem the first time, our chance of success the second time is much higher. Over time, this repeated process will become quicker, and it will seem easier and easier. But only over time, and over many repetitions, and probably with some mistakes and failures mixed in.

HOW MOST OF US DEAL WITH REPEATED CHALLENGE

After overcoming a challenge, we move on immediately, and expect that we will be able to recall any important parts of the solution later. For example:

> Grace has done most of her homework for a class, but the

last question is of a type she doesn't think she has seen before. She tries a few methods suggested by the current chapter, but nothing seems to work. She feels a little anxious, but she decides to give it a break for dinner. Just as she's leaving her room, the solution hits her, based on an obscure method from a previous chapter. She goes back to your desk, finishes the question and finishes her homework, and closes her notebook triumphantly.

Next week, she gets stuck again while working on her homework. She thinks about the problem for a few moments, and no ideas come to mind. But then, she thinks back to the last time she had a mystery problem. She remembers that the solution came to her when she decided to break for dinner. So she decides to do the same thing this time.

But it doesn't seem to work this time. She finishes dinner, returns to her desk, and still there is no solution. There must be something she did last time that worked, but she just can't remember all the details. She's stuck.

That's funny, she thinks. It seemed so obvious at the end last time.

HOW TO BETTER HANDLE REPEATED CHALLENGE

If you want to handle repeated challenge in the best way, you have to start by realizing that the goal isn't to change your challenges. The goal is to improve your ability to handle them.

This takes an extra step or two that we're not used to: reflecting on current successes just after they happen, and leaving notes for your future self to benefit from. Here's how that looks in practice:

Rusty has done most of his homework for a class, but the

last question is of a type he doesn't think he's seen before. He tries a few methods suggested by the current chapter, but nothing seems to work. He feels a little anxious, but he decides to give it a break for dinner. Just as he's leaving his room, the solution hits him, based on an obscure method from a previous chapter. He goes back to his desk, finishes the question and finishes his homework, and closes his notebook triumphantly.

Then, thinking forward to "future Rusty" and the challenges he will have to overcome, he opens his notebook again and spends a few minutes writing down what he just discovered. It comes back in slow motion, and he gets it all down: the feeling of being stuck (so future Rusty can recognize it for what it is more easily later), the ideas he considered and rejected (so future Rusty can get better at analyzing options), the decision to break for dinner (so future Rusty can learn from his lucky experiment of solving a problem by giving it some space), and the flash of insight itself (which, Rusty now realizes, actually came from a mental survey of cryptic hints the teacher had given when assigning the homework).

Now he has it all down.

Next week, Rusty gets stuck again while working on his homework. He thinks about the problem for a few moments, and no ideas come to mind. But then, he remembers that he had this feeling last week. He turns back in his notebook, and reads the notes he left himself a week ago. Suddenly it's much clearer. He goes through the current problem step by step; he reviews what the teacher has said this week; he re-solves last week's problem. He still can't find the answer, but he doesn't worry about that. Instead, he breaks for dinner. He's pretty sure he'll figure it out, even though he doesn't yet know what the solution will be.

Sure enough, while Rusty is eating, he thinks of

something that might work. When he gets back to his desk, he works out the entire idea. It works! He breathes a small sigh of relief.

And then, crucially, he opens his notebook and begin yet another note to "future Rusty."

OKAY, SO WHAT ARE THE STEPS AGAIN?

Whenever you solve a problem that you think you might face again, think forward to what will happen when you are confronted with a similar problem in the future. That will give yourself the idea of *what to do this time*, so that you will be able to take advantage in the future of what you learned just now. So:

1. Think about what you just did
2. Think about what was helpful about it
3. Write a note to your future self

Don't skip that third step! Writing that note to your future self means you don't have to rely on your (let's face it, imperfect) memory.

This habit is a bit like being a time traveler, in a way: once you ask yourself what your future self would want you to do right now, you'll find yourself taking actions that set you up for huge successes. With practice, you'll get these successes again and again.

In this way you can think of yourself as a *team of you*'s: past you's, current you, and future you's, all working together to shape the path to best fit the team (in other words, to best fit you).

SUMMARY

If you want to get good at something over time, you have to analyze your performance. "Reps" alone won't do it.

EXPERT LEVEL

You will face different kinds of repeated challenges in the future. Not just tests and courses, but interviews and jobs, and difficult conversations, and planning for a career and family, and beyond. The same tools apply.

12

INTERLUDE: HOW TO "WIN"

What good is an idea if it remains only an idea?

— SIMON SINEK

WHAT GOOD IS ALL THIS WORK?

LET'S PAUSE for a moment to consider why you're reading this book. "To become a bright (or brighter) student" is the easy answer, of course, but let's look more deeply. What *good* is it to be a bright student? (And, for that matter, what will you do after you've made it that far?)

OUR CULTURAL ASSUMPTIONS

The most common answer in the modern United States has to do with the notion that doing well in secondary school can lead to admission into an exclusive university, which in turn sets one up for a desirable or lucrative career. Hence, being a bright student leads to success and comfort later in life.

Whether broadly true or not, this framing is pervasive. It

drives many decisions made both by and for students starting before high school and lasting throughout their undergraduate careers and even beyond.

There are two key problems with this answer.

1. It frames being a bright student as a particular point you are trying to get to, rather than as an ongoing process, and
2. It often replaces a critical analysis of your options and "best moves" when planning for the years ahead.

A BETTER PERSPECTIVE

Regarding the first problem: as we've seen in Chapter 5, "Harnessing your mindset," and as we'll see again in both Chapter 14, "Trust yourself, trust the process," and Chapter 20, "Be your own pilot," the habits described in this book are intended to be lifelong. Just as with athletic training, you reap the benefits of these habits only for as long as you maintain them.

So, you should avoid the mindset that high school is a series of hoops to jump through, or a collection of checkmarks to get onto your transcript. Instead, think of these years as a time to experiment with and permanently acquire habits that will make you more effective *for your entire life*.

Regarding the second problem: during these years, the best students transition from working in accordance with others' well-meaning and generally wise suggestions, to developing their own internal compass.

So let's acknowledge and embrace the need to develop a framework for setting your own direction, for considering options broadly, and for leveraging not only your strengths but also your savvy.

But let me be blunt: this is an extremely difficult process, and you will fail lots of times. Fortunately, there are many people available to help. When you fail, parents, study partners, teachers, and mentors can all help you to recover and try again.

We'll come back to this again at the end of the book.

∼

SUMMARY

To capably create your own future, you may need something more powerful than the "default" planning process.

13
BITE-SIZED CHUNKS

The difficult, we do immediately. The impossible takes a little longer.

— U. S. ARMY SLOGAN

As you know, breaking problems into small chunks makes them easier overall. The same applies to assignments and projects.

WHY DOES THIS WORK?

One of the main reasons for this is that we all have limited but replenishable attention spans. We can only take in so much information or produce so much output in a sitting. So it's best to work in small sessions, and then to take a break. It's actually a lot like eating. After all, it takes an enormous quantity of food to feed a person for his or her lifetime. But you can eat only the tiniest fraction of that total in a single meal. In the same way, you can both learn and produce an unthinkably vast quantity...but you can only do so a little bit at a time.

Don't fight this natural law. That would be like purposely giving yourself a stomachache from eating too much at once.

Another reason for the need to break projects and assignments into smaller pieces is that it's natural to get discouraged—and therefore less effective—in the face of overwhelm. A large project may seem manageable from a distance, but up close it usually seems more complicated, because of the interactions among the pieces. The closer you get to starting, the more discouraged you can become.

WHAT SHOULD YOU DO?

When first approaching a large project, don't plan to finish it. Instead, aim only to break it down into more-manageable pieces.

A good rule of thumb is to consider how long you expect the project to take in all, then expect to spend *a full third* of that time on the breaking-down process.

Most people find it surprising that organizing a project should take a third of a project's time. After all, isn't doing the project the hard part? Well, no. Doing it and organizing it are both hard, but they're hard in different ways. Make the overall project easier by taking advantage of that difference.

As I mentioned a few chapters ago, at any given moment you are well-suited to certain kinds of tasks but less-well-suited to others. Understanding that projects have two different parts allows you to work on the part you're in the mood to work on. In effect, you get twice as much productivity, because you can better match the work to your mood.

A common objection to this idea is that you have to do the planning before you can "do the doing," but I have found that that is not true. You can do the planning before the work, or you can start the work and get to the planning later. Or you can do a little bit of both. Every bit of work makes the planning easier, and every bit of planning makes the work easier. As long as you're engaged in the part of the project that you feel excited to engage in, you'll do good work no matter where you start.

WHAT OTHER BENEFITS WILL YOU GET?

Another piece of good news is that since you can now better estimate the size of projects, you will be less vulnerable to overwhelm: you can be more realistic right from the start about what it will take to get something done.

Yet another piece of good news is that some people are generally better at organizing, and others are better at doing. Once you better understand your preferences and skills, you have a better chance of successfully teaming up with someone who is better at the part you find most difficult.

Whether you find someone else to work with or not, you'll find that your skills as a worker and your skills as a self-manager reinforce and amplify each other. Unlike most people, you can start building the self-management part now, instead of waiting until much later in life.

SUMMARY

Break projects up into small chunks. Give yourself time to do this.

14

TRUST YOURSELF, TRUST THE PROCESS

It always seems impossible until it's done.

— NELSON MANDELA

IN THIS CHAPTER you'll learn how to do very difficult things. Maybe even things that people think are impossible.

First, let's be clear on what impossible means. I don't mean a problem that you don't know a solution for. I mean *a problem you're not even sure can be solved.*

HOW TO DO THE IMPOSSIBLE

The most important thing you can do is make sure that your mind keeps at it. That's important because in this situation the mind usually wants to give up as soon as possible. And that creates a vicious cycle: the problem seems tough; the mind gives up; the problem goes unsolved; the impossibility of the problem is confirmed.

That cycle is all just a mind game, and you have much

more control over the outcome than you realize. Here are the five steps to keeping your mind on your side in these situations:

1. *Accept calmly* that the problem seems difficult or even impossible.
2. Note the difference between *seeming* difficult and actually *being* difficult. Difficult-seeming problems are scary, but scaring you is their only power over you, and you can avoid that. (Problems that are *actually* difficult are wonderful: they are our best chance to grow. Reread Chapter 5, "Harnessing your mindset," if that surprises you.)
3. Trust that any challenging problem will teach you something worth knowing.
4. Trust that any challenging problem, however devious it appears to be, is actually fair and solvable.
5. Take it in small steps.

STEP 1: AVOID FIGHT-OR-FLIGHT

Calm acceptance of the problem can be the hardest part. Difficult things can feel like crises, and crises feel urgent.

In some rare cases, this reaction is helpful. For example, if you were confronted with a lion in the jungle, you wouldn't pause to reflect. Your body would panic, and you would run automatically.

But most problems aren't lions. A crisis reaction is rarely helpful. No matter how panic-worthy a problem may seem, it is rarely more than words on a page, or an issue in your mind. Any reaction your body has is misplaced, however real the reaction may seem in the moment. You can train yourself to step back, recognize the situation for what it really is, and consider your next steps calmly.

Finding patience in these moments does not feel natural for most people. It takes a lot of practice. But it can be done, and you can get better at this. Starting today.

If this is the part you have the most trouble with, I recommend that you learn a bit more about meditation. Most meditation practices improve this skill. And there are more easy ways to start these days than ever before, including an ever-growing collection of smartphone apps for beginners.

STEP 2: DELAY JUDGMENT FOR A MINUTE

It's helpful to pause and consider a problem before trying to solve it. Unfortunately, most people start trying to solve a problem before they're even finished understanding what the problem is! So they fall into the bad habit of judging problems by whether they can be solved instantly. When it looks hard, many students make an instantaneous and unconscious decision to be scared.

Quit trying to judge so fast. Give it a minute, think it through, and work at it for a few minutes before you decide anything. Remember, between "trivial" and "impossible" is a wonderful level of difficulty called "I don't know yet," where a problem tests and stretches your mind's powers, exercising and strengthening it just by giving it something worth working on. But in order to get these benefits, you have to give yourself some time and space. So don't try to judge. Just give it a chance.

STEP 3: DIFFICULT PROBLEMS MAKE YOU SMARTER

The point of a difficult problem isn't just to solve it; part of the point is to become a better solver by grappling with it.

The longer you engage with a problem, the smarter you become as a result. So don't despair when a problem captures your attention for a long time. Instead, be glad that your mind is getting such a good workout.

STEP 4: REMEMBER, THE PROBLEM IS SOLVABLE

All problems are fair and solvable. (A fair problem is one that can be solved, using only information you already have.)

This advice can be heartbreaking, because it's actually a lie: some problems really aren't fair. But it serves you well to assume that they are, for the simple reason that most minds can't work effectively on problems they believe to be unfair. In fact, one of the easiest ways to get someone to give up on a problem is to convince him or her that the problem has no solution. And yet we undermine ourselves in exactly this way, all the time. When you're grappling with a challenge, it's the easiest thing in the world to let ourselves off the hook by entertaining doubt that the question can ever be answered. Resist this natural urge. Instead, insist that the problem can be solved, and that you will solve it.

STEP 5: ALL YOU REALLY NEED TO DO IS START

Here we bring the lofty ideas of the earlier steps down to the level of "action plan." This is crucial because believing that you'll come up with an answer only helps if you then have some idea of how to start looking. Here's how: *just start*. Even if 90% of the question is completely unknown to you, working at the 10% that seems possible really is enough. Once you have that 10% solved, you'll most likely have an idea of what to try next. (And by the way, the 10% you start with can be the beginning of the problem, the end of the problem, or something from the middle. It doesn't matter:

start anywhere you can, and just trust that everything will work out as you go along.)

SUMMARY

Extremely difficult problems are difficult in part because of false assumptions people commonly have about them. Solving these problems requires a different approach. That approach can be learned.

15
IMPROVE THE QUESTION

Temporarily avoiding the hard part of a problem will allow you to make progress, and may shed light on the difficulties.

— PAUL ZEITZ

IF AT FIRST YOU DON'T SUCCEED, CHANGE THE RULES

SOMETIMES, when you're trying to tackle a difficult problem —and this can mean anything from a hard question in a math competition to trying to figure out the best way to prepare for a job interview—you will have no idea where to even start. One of the most important techniques for getting to an answer in this situation is to *improve the question*. That is, change the question to an easier one.

The idea is that while you may not be able to solve the problem at hand, you can probably solve a simpler version of the same problem. Eliminate some of the complications or change the parameters. Anything to make the problem solvable.

Once you solve the improved version, you add the original

complications back in one by one, re-solving each version of the problem. (This is basically a variant on breaking the problem into bite-sized chunks, except that you start with the largest easily-solvable chunk you can, and then add on from there.)

This is a style of thinking that takes some getting used to. It will only help a little bit at first, but the more familiar with it you become, the (vastly) more powerful this technique will make you.

After some practice, you'll discover that you are comfortable adjusting the difficulty of a problem smoothly; this is sometimes called "moving along the difficulty gradient." Once you can do this easily, you'll find that the actual solving part isn't nearly as hard as it used to be.

Let's look at a few examples of this technique in action.

IMPROVING A MATH QUESTION

> We're going to play a simple coin flipping game. We take turns flipping a fair coin. The first one to get "heads" wins. You go first. What's your chance of winning?

Unless you're most of the way through an advanced probability class, this question is very difficult. At least at first.

But let's try to change the question to make it easier. Let's change the game to only last one "round": You take a turn, then I take a turn, and that's all. In that case, you'd have a 50% chance of winning, because you'd have a 50/50 chance of of getting a heads on your flip. In order for me to win, I'd need you to get a tails, and then I'd need a heads. That gives me a 25% chance of winning.

Okay, that's progress, and it gives us an idea of what question to ask next: what about making the game last for *two* rounds? Like we said, in the first round, you have a 50% of winning and I have a 25% chance of winning. If you do a bit of calculation, you realize that in the second round you have twice as much chance of winning as I do, just like in the first round. If we extend it to three rounds, the same thing happens in the third round: your chance of winning is always twice mine.

Well, if your chance of winning is twice mine *in each round*, then your chance of winning must be twice mine *overall*. So your overall chance of winning must be 2/3 and mine must be 1/3, since those are the only numbers for which one is twice as big as the other, and they add up to 100% (which they have to, since it is 100% certain that *someone* will win, eventually.)

We solved a hard question by answering a series of easier ones. We started by answering a simple question, and we added the complications back in, one at a time, until we found ourselves answering the original question.

IMPROVING A LIFE QUESTION

> Which colleges should I apply to, and how will I apply to them and get into one, during a very busy junior year?

This question is hard in a different way from the last one. But again, let's change the question to make it easier.

Let's change the question to only be about three target colleges: "ABCC," a local community college; "X State," a state school about two hours' drive from your home; and "Harmouth," a well-regarded private school far away.

You don't really know anything about ABCC, except that your friend's brother went there. X State is a popular choice for people from your high school. You think Harmouth is expensive and hard to get in to, and its name keeps turning up on the Internet.

Two questions that turn up right away are: which place will you enjoy more, and which place will give your more opportunities later in life? Now that we have specific questions, we can start research. So, you talk to your friend's brother and discover that he is now a successful local plumber. He tells you about his time at ABCC, what he liked and didn't, and about his job today. Then, you talk to your high school guidance counselor about X State. Because of what you know about ABCC, you are able to ask better questions, and you learn about a few people who went to X State from your high school, some of whom only discovered what they wanted to study after being at X State for a year or more. Finally, you do some online research and find that many people who go to Harmouth mostly wind up working for large law firms where they are very busy, and that it takes them some years of work to pay off their tuition bills.

As in the case of the math question above, simplifying the question has helped right from the start. You are already learning what kinds of things make schools different, and you are learning to ask yourself questions that will matter to the final decision: Do you want to live near home, or move away? Does a high-pressure job sound intimidating or invigorating? How close are you to knowing what you want to study at college, or do after college?

As you answer those questions, you can probably decide which of the original three options looks best to you. Let's say it's "X State." Great. Now you can look around for other state schools in the region and work through this process again. Only this time, you have better questions to ask, and more confidence with the process.

By the time you have an idea which schools look really good, figuring out how to apply will be much less complicated. And, as a bonus, because of all the work you did, you'll probably be a stronger candidate. After all, you'll be a better-informed and more accomplished applicant after all that thinking and research.

Note: I don't mean that you should do all research without help. I just mean that making a problem simpler helps you get started, and starting helps you learn the things you'll need in order to finish.

∼

SUMMARY

Hard problems are often best solved by first solving easier versions of the same problem.

16

STRUGGLE WITH THE EARLY MATERIAL

Being a student is easy. But learning requires actual work.

— WILLIAM CRAWFORD

EASY ISN'T ALWAYS BETTER

WE'D LOVE for everything to be easy. But we're misguided. Sometimes "easy" actually just doesn't work as well as "difficult" does.

There are two ways in which this is true. The first is the most general: difficult work cues the brain to pay extra attention. Therefore it's especially helpful to challenge yourself, in order to get the most out of your brain. (There's a lot to say about this, but I'll leave that aside for now.)

The second is that we often confuse memorizing and learning. Memorizing, which is the act of committing facts to memory, is relatively easy. Sure, it takes time, but it's straightforward and predictable. Learning, on the other hand, is quite difficult, unpredictable, and effortful.

FRAMEWORKS MATTER MOST

Here's why: learning is not actually about acquiring new knowledge. It's more about about figuring out how to file that knowledge away: how to think about it, and what to connect it to. In other words, learning is mostly the process of *building mental frameworks* ("schemata") for knowledge and processes. Building these frameworks, these schemata, is the part of learning that is most valuable, and feels hardest.

This is why I told you earlier to annotate books as you read. It's also a big part of why taking notes is useful, even if you throw away the notes. Just figuring out how to write something down is an important part of putting it into your mind in a way that fits well with everything else you already have up there.

You should also be aware that as you get older, your learning process will shift from being less and less about creating brand-new schemata, and more and more about modifying schemata you already have. When people talk about "the value of experience" and sometimes even "wisdom," they are talking at least in part about this ability of older people to rely on already-present schemata to give them a huge learning advantage.

An important implication is that a teacher's ability to teach you something is limited by the teacher's ability to speak, work, and think with your schemata (i.e. to *be like you*). You have certain schemata in place already, some of which the teacher doesn't have, and you are "missing" others that the teacher would like you to have. Unfortunately, many teachers aren't even aware that their schemata are different from yours.

In other words, some teachers think that everyone has the *same mental frameworks*, but with *different knowledge* filling those frameworks. So, they set out to give you knowledge. Which, it turns out, doesn't work all that well.

Very good teachers recognize that their job is to help you get the right mental frameworks, and that once you have the right frameworks in place, acquiring knowledge to fill that framework is the easiest thing in the world.

FIGURE OUT THE BASICS FIRST

Now, you might not have control of who your teachers are, but you do have control of how you learn. So, when something doesn't make sense to you, ask yourself (or the teacher): *how should I be thinking about this?*

If that doesn't work, ask this instead: *"What are the most basic ideas I should understand about this topic?"* In general, teachers know what the "basic ideas" of any topic are, and once you understand those ideas, really understand them, you'll find that the more advanced ideas in the subject aren't actually that hard.

To put it more plainly: most teachers hurry through the beginning material so that they can "get to the interesting stuff" later on. But when you're a great student, you know better. You concentrate enormously on the basic material. You make sure you completely understand it forwards, backwards, and sideways. You don't stop until can use it fluidly and gracefully. It takes you longer to get started this way, and it requires both you and your teacher to have some extra patience. But once you have that part down, you probably won't need much more of the teacher's help.

Doing things this way ensures that you are *building appropriate schemata* for thinking about the subject, rather than just memorizing facts about it. So spend lots of energy and practice time on the first few weeks' material in any class, and you will be delighted to discover that the rest of the class doesn't feel as difficult to you as it does to everyone else.

By the way, have you ever noticed that most classes take a few weeks to "ramp up" from "intro speed" to "full speed"? I don't know whether this is why, but I do know that that pattern helps you to follow this advice.

SUMMARY

Faster isn't necessarily better.

17

WORK LIKE AN EXPERT

If we do only what is required of us, we are slaves; the moment we do more, we are free.

— CICERO

Now that you know the importance of learning the basics, pay attention to how *learning the advanced stuff is different*.

Some people never figure out this difference. They have some success learning the first lessons of a subject, and then they form a habit of "protecting" their knowledge of the basics against new information that could threaten what they "know." (See Chapter 5, "Harnessing your mindset," to remind yourself how this can happen.)

By contrast, you will instead maintain a growth mindset (also known as "beginner's mind"), which means thinking of your knowledge as *a way to get to expertise*, rather than thinking of it as an accomplishment.

CONCEPTS, TOOLS, SKILLS

When you're doing it right, it goes like this: first you get the *concepts*, then you get the *expert tools*, then you develop *skill* with the tools.

For example, when you learn physics, one of the things you discover early on is the idea of "projectile motion," which is the name for the way things move when they are flying through the air. Once you understand this *concept*, you learn the equations that govern this behavior. These equations are the *tools* that let you predict exactly where a flying thing will land, and when.

But the really interesting learning happens next. That's where you transition from knowing all the stuff, to understanding how to use it effectively.

Once you've gained those expert *skills*, word problems become not just doable, but obvious. You'll watch baseball and *see* what it means for an outfielder to "be where the ball is going to land." This is a practical framework for seeing the world that you can learn after you know the concepts, and have had some practice with the tools. But you don't get this framework automatically. You still have to work for it.

A FEW EXAMPLES

Let's see how people do this in practice—both correctly and incorrectly—through a few general examples.

Consider people trying to learn, say, precalculus. They often spend their time memorizing formulas. But you now understand that although formulas are necessary for understanding math, they aren't enough. Formulas are only *tools*. They only make sense after you've learned the basic concepts that they govern. And once you've learned the formulas and read the explanations, you need to transition to learning the expert skills. In the case of math, this skill comes from solving problems. By trying (and, usually, failing a lot), people learn a lot more useful precalculus a lot more quickly.

What about people trying to learn a language? They usually start with memorizing vocabulary. Of course, you have to know what the words mean before you can start putting them together in any useful way. (This is the basic *concept* of learning a foreign language: as Steve Martin said, "They have a different word for everything!"). The most common mistake here is to try to memorize all the vocabulary at the beginning. What's smarter is to get a small collection of vocabulary words down cold, then start reading, speaking, and writing in the target language using that implied vocabulary. By doing this, you work the necessary skills (reading, speaking, writing) that are built on the fundamental tools (meanings of words), as soon as possible. Fluency then becomes possible.

Sports also have their drills that lead to mastery of the basic patterns of movement and attention required for success (as well as general conditioning). Once you have these tools, you can (and should) immediately start building the skills needed to play the sport; through play, you might eventually begin to win.

HOW WE USUALLY GO WRONG… AND HOW TO DO BETTER

Each subject has its fundamental knowledge that must be completely committed to memory before mastery becomes possible. But each subject will also allow you to keep working on the fundamentals instead of graduating to the skills of mastery, if you're not careful.

That's why it's important not to confuse the fundamentals with the skills that are meant to be built *on top of* the fundamentals.

Why would we keep working on fundamentals? The

answer's simple. It's because it's always comfortable to work at something you're already good at. It's harder to work at something new. So, if you want to master a subject, there comes a point at which you need to decide that you've mastered the necessary core knowledge, then tear yourself away from working at the fundamentals, and start working at a new, higher level.

And this is why many successful language-acquisition programs insist that students begin speaking as soon as they have a minimum vocabulary. It's also why math is best learned by solving problems rather than by reading explanations. (And it's why no one's ever gotten good at a sport by watching it from the bleachers.)

As soon as you can, you have to transition from learning more fundamentals to *practicing*. And that means *learning from your mistakes*.

DELIBERATE PRACTICE

Anders Ericsson (mentioned earlier, in Chapter 3, "10,000 hours?") describes the idea of *deliberate practice* – an effort to systematically practice just beyond one's skill level – as the key to accelerated improvement in any discipline. This sort of deliberate practice is difficult and demoralizing, as it involves constant failure. And it can be exhausting, because it challenges your mind at multiple levels at once. Not only are you grappling with uncomfortable new processes and techniques, but you are also monitoring your own process, and devising new challenges for yourself on the fly. So, it's hard. But *it works like nothing else*.

When you are preparing for a test, you must begin taking practice tests as soon as you can reasonably expect to be able to answer some of the questions asked. As you struggle with the material, you will not only learn which bits of fundamental knowledge you are missing; you'll also learn whether your pace is correct, whether your nerves are hurting or helping you, at what time of day you do your best work, how much sleep you need, and on and on and on.

With each mistake, you have an opportunity to be completely honest about the reasons for your error, which in turn leads to ideas about how to correct future errors by changing not only your knowledge, but also your habits and even your outlook.

Obviously, this is not the same as just "doing" an activity. For example, playing a sport for fun for eight hours a day is not the same as deliberate practice; deliberate practice would involve setting up drills to specifically focus on deficiencies in one's skill, and practicing those drills until the deficiency is corrected.

Ericsson draws the conclusion that natural talent means nothing without deliberate practice. In fact, in situations where we think of somebody having natural talent, an investigation shows that they just got started on their deliberate practice earlier than most.

When you want to get good at something, aim to do it the way masters do it. Then, when you fail, be gentle and honest with yourself. Look for exactly what you did wrong, observing yourself without judgment. Then address the mistakes, whatever they may turn out to be.

SUMMARY

Mastery of the basics is just the beginning.

18

STEERING THE SUPERTANKER

Motivation is what gets you started. Habit is what keeps you going.

— JIM RYUN

CONSIDER A SUPERTANKER: a monstrously huge and heavy ship carrying an enormous quantity of (very heavy) cargo. The goal of the ship is to move through many miles of open ocean as efficiently as possible.

The captain of such a supertanker finds him- or herself in a tricky situation: it takes a very long time to get the thing to turn or to change speeds. There's just so much *mass* there, so much inertia, and the engines and rudders are comparatively small. Sure, it can move pretty fast, but it takes a really long time to get up to speed. And once it's going in a straight line, getting it to turn can take a very long time.

So driving this thing requires considerable foresight and planning.

But one thing it doesn't require is a lot of force. The captain doesn't have to apply much effort at all to get the ship to turn. He or she just turns the captain's wheel, and the ship will (eventually) turn. Even if the captain is willing to put enormous effort into it, it doesn't really matter: the wheel isn't *hard* to turn, and forcing it doesn't really help anything. It just takes a long time.

The captain needs planning and patience, not strength.

HOW THIS APPLIES TO YOU

Consider a human: a creature who lives for tens of thousands of days, yet experiences life in seconds, minutes, and hours. The captain of this "ship" is making decisions in the moment that will have their biggest effects only much later. The crisis of the moment is resolved mainly through decisions made in the past. Sound familiar?

It's enormously helpful to think of ourselves as supertankers. But we aren't hard to steer because we have lots of mass; we are hard to steer because of our *habits,* which keep us moving more or less in a straight line. The inertia of our habits can only be overcome through patience and consistence, not effort and struggle.

The winning strategy is a small but consistent effort applied over a long time.

ONLY THE SMALLEST CHANGES STICK

Consider New Year's resolutions and the like: "this time I'm going to do things differently." Setbacks and ambition alike often lead to grand promises to ourselves, pacts that we imagine will create a new and improved self.

But in practice, only the smallest changes stick. Never "I'll do three hours of homework a night from now on" but rather "from now on, I'll spend three minutes per night double-checking my work afterwards." Small changes are much more manageable.

Small changes also create a slightly different self-perspective, a shifted vision of self that can accommodate the next small changes more easily. When you make a small change, you're exploiting a well-understood psychological principle known as the "foot in the door" phenomenon: people tend to agree to a large request after first agreeing to a small request. (And yes, it works on yourself just fine.) In this case, asking yourself for a small change makes it easier to accept another (even larger) change later.

But trying to start with a big change generally doesn't work at all.

SMALL DECISIONS CREATE BIG IMPROVEMENTS

It seems to me what powers this phenomenon is that we all like to feel that we are reasonable people, operating from self-consistent principles. So, once you've accepted (for example) that spending three minutes checking your homework is a good idea, the mostly-unconscious parts of your mind that try to keep you internally consistent and reasonable get to work. They raise questions like "isn't checking one's work a sign of thoroughness?" and "how else might I be more thorough?" and "aren't thorough people especially good students?" and "what other things do especially good students do that I might enjoy?" and so forth. Again, this happens mostly on an unconscious level, so you just experience your habits "just improving for no reason." But in fact, they did improve for a reason. They improved because of a small positive change that you set in motion. It all started with a decision that seemed tiny at the time.

START NOW, THEN BE PATIENT

This all sounds good, but does it really work in the modern world? Here, everything happens fast, and it all keeps getting faster. By some estimates, even the rate of the acceleration itself is increasing: write a computer program now, and have it running minutes later; by tomorrow it can be on a million phones or more. Make an online purchase and have it delivered to you in hours or even minutes. The witticism "instant gratification takes too long" begins to seem like a valid complaint.

So of course everyone expects this instantaneous timetable to apply to everything, even to their own self-improvement.

When we can't adopt a new habit within minutes, we're tempted to think that something might be wrong with us. When we make a mistake, we expect to be able to instantly analyze it, understand what we did wrong, and fix it on the spot so that we'll never make that mistake again. If we can't, something feels wrong, and we aim to try to process faster for next time — in effect, applying more force to the wheel, trying to get the ship to turn faster.

But in truth, humans don't work that way, can't work that way, and may never be able to work that way. It takes time to change, much longer than we'd like, and with every generation—perhaps even with every decade, or less—the timescale for human change drifts further and further out of sync with the timescale of other kinds of development and evolution in our technologies and in other parts of our daily lives.

The disconnect between the timescale for human change and the timescale for other changes causes enormous trouble unless it is recognized and accounted for.

There are two important things you simply must keep in

mind if you are to create meaningful and lasting changes (i.e. improvements) in yourself:

You must *be patient with yourself*. Change will happen far more slowly than you expect. Impatience creates frustration, and frustration prevents you from adopting the mental states you need in order to improve meaningfully. (See Chapter 14, "Trust yourself, trust the process," for more help with being patient.)

You must also *start now*. Take whatever step you can readily take. *Starting small is good enough.* No need to be overly ambitious about it.

Finally, here are two ways people often get this wrong. Avoid these mistakes:

1. Giving up too soon

When you want to make a change in yourself, you generally take some action or actions intended to create that change. But often, you'll see no change at all—at least not at first. The common, but incorrect, response is to give up.

Sometimes this mistake comes from fear that the action or change can't be achieved (see Chapter 14, "Trust yourself, trust the process"). And sometimes this mistake comes from underestimating just how slowly change occurs. It takes what seems like forever.

Stick with it for at least three times as long as you think it will take, and only then decide: are you seeing any change at all in the desired direction? If so, keep it up.

If it feels like too much effort for too little change, remember that changes that take an extraordinarily long time to create *also take an extraordinarily long time to undo once they are in place.* Making changes in yourself is like steering a supertanker: even small changes at the steering wheel create huge changes in where the ship ends up later. It's just that it takes a long time to get there.

2. Oversteering

Oversteering happens when you attempt to make some change, fail to observe any (or enough) benefit as a result, and assume that what you're doing isn't enough, and so you double down on the change. This case is perhaps not as bad as giving up too soon, but it's still pretty bad: you wind up causing yourself unnecessary frustration, and you may even give up on the method entirely. As I said before: "forcing the wheel" doesn't help…and it can tire you out.

Instead of forcing the wheel, aim to keep changes small, and stick with them for three times as long as you think they'll need.

∽

SUMMARY (IN VERSE)

> *"Sow a thought, reap an action;*
> *sow an action, reap a habit;*
> *sow a habit, reap a character;*
> *sow a character, reap a destiny."*

19

DARE: DEVISE, ADJUST, REPEAT, EXECUTE

It does not matter how slowly you go, as long as you do not stop.

— CONFUCIUS

THE IDEAS in this book are meant to be turned into habits. In fact, the process of becoming a better student—indeed, a better person—is the process of *developing better habits*, plain and simple. You will not always have the willpower to do the right thing, the smart thing, the effective thing; but you will always have the willpower to *do what you are used to doing*. Thus, the key is to sculpt what you are used to doing.

Unfortunately, forming a new habit is generally more difficult than simply resolving to do something in a different way from now on. Not only do we overcommit to our changes (see Chapter 18, "Steering the supertanker"), but we also have a hard time making appropriate adjustments to these habits as we build on them over time.

So, try this four-step process for adopting and shaping a new habit:

DEVISE

Pick something you'd like to change and dream up a way in which you could improve. For example, if your goal is to be better-rested, then you might devise the habit of going to bed 30 minutes earlier than you're used to.

You can think of this step as writing a recipe.

Try doing it once.

ADJUST

After trying it once, evaluate what happened. Did it work? Was it difficult? Did it throw something else off?

Take a few minutes to write down the parts that worked well and the parts that didn't, along with ideas for improving. Also, write down how it benefited you, as well as how it felt uncomfortable. Finally, note what other things (if any) got thrown off as a result of the experiment.

For example, you may have found that getting to bed early was stressful because you couldn't easily finish your homework, but that the next day at school was easier and more enjoyable. You may have felt that getting to sleep would have been easier had you eaten a lighter dinner. You may find that reading a few pages of a novel helps you transition from merely being in bed to actually being asleep. And so on.

Now, adjust your plan for next time: make little changes that will make the experiment easier, more effective, more pleasant, with fewer bad side effects.

Write down this new way of doing it.

You can think of this step as improving the recipe.

REPEAT

In the previous steps, you've been trying a new habit on for size. At each step you've probably been spending part of your attention on how to do it, and whether it's working the way you want it to.

In this step, you've got it pretty well ironed out, and you're just doing it once to make sure you can put it more or less on auto-pilot.

In this example, putting it on auto-pilot might mean deciding to go to bed early every day next week. Just to make sure you can do it without a lot of extra thought or effort.

You can think of this step as trying the recipe without having to think about it.

EXECUTE

In this step you decide the schedule on which you're going to run this new habit on auto-pilot. Also, you'll put it into your calendar (or whatever you use to plan your days).

The common wisdom is that you should schedule to do this at least thirty times (and perhaps as many as a hundred) before you can safely consider this habit locked in to your routine. What this really means is that you should not try to have too many habits "in the pipeline" at once.

SUMMARY

Creating new habits is important. Don't leave it to chance. Instead, use this method, or one like it.

EXPERT LEVEL

Once you've done these four steps a few times, I recommend you read Charles Duhigg's excellent book <u>The Power of Habit</u> for the advanced course in changing your routines and thereby improving your abilities.

20
BE YOUR OWN PILOT

Should you fail to pilot your own ship, don't be surprised at what inappropriate port you find yourself docked.

— TOM ROBBINS

The more decisions that you are forced to make alone, the more you are aware of your freedom to choose.

— THORNTON WILDER

A good plan violently executed now is better than a perfect plan executed next week.

— GEORGE S. PATTON

EARLIER YOU READ about the importance of a *framework for setting your own direction*. I'll explore that in more detail now.

GETTING HELP

As you may have noticed, making important life decisions is mostly regarded by our culture as something best left to the experts: first your parents make decisions for you, then college counselors, then graduate advisors, then professional mentors and managers, and on and on and on.

This isn't necessarily such a bad thing: experience often leads to better results. (Also, there are certain kinds of mental tasks related to decision-making that become biologically easier after one's early 20's, so advisors for students may be especially helpful.)

Sometimes these experts will be amazing professionals with fantastic, groundbreaking advice for you. On the other hand, sometimes they'll just be a "safety net" of decent advice, so your very worst decisions won't be too bad. You need to be able to tell the difference.

Ultimately, you'd prefer to make your own decisions, perhaps informed by the wisdom of others, but not defined by it or by them.

GOING IT ALONE

Most decisions are informed by your "autopilot." You make decisions at least partly (if not entirely) by seeing that the current situation matches some past situation (possibly in relevant ways, and possibly not), and then doing in the present whatever you think was the right thing to do in the past. (See Gladwell's Blink and Kahneman's Thinking, Fast and Slow for more in-depth knowledge on this.) This is not a bad thing, but it's useful to understand how to balance this important but unconscious force with your conscious, executive mind.

Also, understand that your conscious mind can have arguments with itself. Aligning your identity, your emotions, and your cognition behind a single decision can be hard work. For example, there might be disagreement between what you want, what you *think* you want, and what you *want* to want. It's so complicated that it can be hard to get started. But at this point in the book, you're no longer afraid of complications.

A good system can help you overcome these difficulties. Through practice, you'll come to better understand how to align these drives within yourself. The process of making decisions will become easier.

I recommend you find a system that you like. To get you started, I'll provide one of my own.

Mine is a method for making decisions that helps balance your mind, heart, and gut. So it avoids a lot of the problems with "unbalanced" decision making. However, it takes a long time to get really good at it, so think of this as a long-term project. If you give this a try for now, and keep up with it, then sooner or later this method will become part of what makes you especially capable. (Or, at least, it will help you figure out what other system works even better for you.)

It works on problems big ("What should I do with my life?") and small ("How can I solve this difficult homework problem?"). I call it the **Pilot Program**.

Before we too far into it, let me acknowledge that there are many, many excellent processes out there for setting and achieving goals. There are two ways in which the Pilot Program is different from most:

1. It uses a *"ready, fire, aim"* strategy. This means that you start quickly, even before you have all the details worked out, and you fine-tune everything

later. This strategy helps you avoid overwhelm and perfectionism, and it helps you build momentum fast. Yet it's also accurate over the long run, because of the fine-tuning that is built into the system.
2. The focus of the Pilot is on *constant improvement*, which allows it to transcend mere goals and aim for more powerful targets: *vision* and *values*. As a result, the Pilot Program is not limited to short-term projects, but rather can be applied on a large scale—as large as you can imagine.

THE FIVE PARTS OF THE PILOT PROGRAM

The five parts of the Pilot Program are: a *Desire*, an *Action List*, a *Journaling Plan*, *Course Correction*, and a *Finish Line*.

Desire: What I want to have achieved, what I want to have, what I want to have done, or what I want to be.

Action List: Specific actions I should take in order to get closer to that vision.

Journaling Plan: The location of my notes on my progress, and my schedule for reviewing the notes.

Course Correction: The actions I should take in order to fine-tune all five of these parts, as I gain experience by doing them.

Finish Line: How I'll be able to tell that I've succeeded.

∽

A QUICK EXAMPLE

Here's a quick example of how this might work:

Desire

To be a straight-A student.

Action List

- Discover some things that straight-A students do, that is different from what I am used to doing
- Identify one that I can't easily do
- Learn how to do that thing
- Turn that learning into habits

Journaling Plan

Every week, I write down in an online journal what I've done during the week that is likely to raise my grades. After journaling, I read through the whole journal from the beginning, and I congratulate myself for the things I have done well.

Course Correction

Then I do three things:

1. Decide whether I am finished learning my latest new habit. If I am, then discover/identify a new one, per my Action List.
2. Make any changes to the Desire, Journaling Plan, Action List, Course Correction, or Finish Line, according to my best judgment at the time.
3. Write notes telling myself what I should try to do the following week in order to stay on target.

Finish Line

I have a report card containing nothing but A's for the current grading period.

~

A LIFE-SIZE QUESTION

Now let's say you're trying to figure out what to do with your life. That's an awfully big question! But the size of the question isn't a problem. Here's how it might work:

Desire

To know what I want to do with my life.

Action List

- Ask some older people what they do, and whether they like it
- Think about what they say and how it applies to me

Journaling Plan

I record all the interviews, and after each one I listen to it again and take notes, focusing on how I think the ideas in that interview apply to me (or not).

Course Correction

I think about which interviews seem most and least helpful, and I use that information to determine what sort of person to try to interview next.

Finish Line

I have written down a specific "Life Goal" that I believe is worth pursuing.

A RESEARCH PROJECT

Here's a different way in which someone might use the Pilot Program to come up with a Life Goal:

Desire

To know what I want to do with my life.

Action List

- Ask myself what I want to do
- Pay attention to what I find myself saying

Journaling Plan

Every time I ask myself the question, I come up with a one-sentence answer and write it down on a piece of paper taped to my wall.

Course Correction

Once a month, I spend ten minutes reading the paper and remembering what made me give each of those answers.

Finish Line

I have noticed myself giving the same answer three or more times. That answer is my Life Goal.

∽

As you can see, two different people could use this method to solve the same problem, and wind up with very different paths and very different results.

Let me be clear: the method isn't easy. You have to really think about each of the parts, and that takes time. Sometimes, it also requires courage.

But the personal attention you put into it is also a major strength of the Pilot Program. Since the parts all come from you, they aren't nearly as vulnerable to anyone else's bias. You are making all the decisions. You are also deciding the very rules of the game. This means that your decisions using this method are more likely to have *high integrity*. In other words, your decisions will be true to yourself. You get to *decide* how much "outside bias" you're going to let in to your process.

Let me suggest some guidelines for deciding how much bias to let in, and how to avoid that bias when you want to.

HOW MUCH BIAS

A good guideline is **replicability**: if many people before you have gotten what you want, and it's clear how they did it, it's probably best to let others' guidance help you. This can mean researching how to do it, or trusting an expert to help you find the best path. Note: this doesn't mean to relinquish all control (or worse, responsibility for the outcome); it just means that you'll probably do better with advice than without.

By contrast, if the result has not been replicated many times, or if it isn't clear how it's been done in the past, then you may be the best guide for your own process, because (1) you care more than anyone else, and (2) you probably know yourself better than anyone else. (One key exception: one or both of your parents might be even better guides than you yourself are.)

Another good guideline is **boundedness**: problems and questions that are well-defined, short-term, multiple-choice, and/or straightforward are usually best answered with outside help or bias. However, more nebulous, long-term, open-ended and difficult-to-even-define problems and questions usually benefit from removing as much bias as possible from the decision process.

One last thing: it's okay to use one method now and another later. For example, many people enlist the help of a college counselor (high bias, high expertise) to figure out where to go to college, and only later use their own process (low bias, high integrity) to determine what sort of career to build on the foundation of the college career.

HOW TO AVOID BIAS

Read through each line you've written as part of your Pilot Program. Ask yourself: why is this here? Whenever you have a hard time answering that question, find and remove the bias.

HOW BIAS CAN HELP

The form of any question or problem often gives you some idea about what kinds of solutions would be appropriate.

For most problems, there are solutions that are considered "out of bounds." That is: there's a strong sense of what you are "allowed" and "not allowed" to do. For example, take the SAT. There, it is not considered valid to write in your own answer choice on the multiple-choice sections. This means that most problems carry with them implicit hints about how the problems should be solved. As you learn to recognize bias, you will learn to recognize solution "hints."

One other way in which bias can help is that it can show you what everyone else has tried, so that you can try doing the opposite. Some very successful companies, for example, got their starts by trying to do what was considered at the time to be "obviously" impossible or crazy.

HOW ELIMINATING BIAS CAN HELP

At its most extreme, the Pilot Program helps you to examine all the possibilities. Even the "crazy" and "impossible" ones. So make sure you take advantage of that leeway by including all the "outside the box" possibilities in your analysis.

∽

SUMMARY

Making your own decisions is actually a lot harder than it sounds. A reliable method helps. Here's one such method. Getting good at it (or at any other) really pays off.

EXPERT LEVEL

Once you get comfortable doing this, try removing the explicit Desire and Finish Line from a project, and continue only with the Action List, Journaling Plan, and Course Correction.

You'll often find that an area of self-improvement is made much more powerful by removing the "fixed destinations" from your thinking and framework, and instead, putting your focus on open-

ended, continuous improvement. This is related to the mindsets described in Chapter 5 ("Harnessing your mindset").

Creating the habit of continual improvement, where you always focus on your next step (Action List, Journaling Plan, Course Correction) is one of the most powerful meta-habits you can build.

EPILOGUE

THIS BOOK IS ONLY INTENDED to get you started. But getting started is enough. If you are now on the path to self-improvement, then all you have to do is stay on the path, and keep moving. I am confident that in time you will learn all I know about academic accomplishment, and more.

But as a culture we're in our second decade of waiting "just a little longer" for automated and customized education to become reality, as though just getting started *weren't* enough. We expect complete perfection and comprehensive self-improvement, and we want it immediately.

Yet such perfection remains distant, as with each new innovation we gain a deeper understanding of just what education at its best really is: a humble and personal communication from one mind to another of what works, or at least of what worked for one person and might work for another.

This is not a failing of technology, and it's not a failing of research. Instead, it's a natural outgrowth of two conflicting schemas: on one hand, we've come to expect the assembly-line industrialization of most every aspect of our modern lives, including education. On the other, we're beginning to realize that no two minds think alike, nor should they be made to, except insofar as is necessary for communication. This flies in the face of some of the assumptions undergirding our recent technological leaps.

Education neither can nor should reduce us all to interchangeable parts, and therefore it cannot scale like so much science and industry. It is personal, not scaleable; sloppy, not tidy; and artisanal, not mere craftwork.

Even so: it can *already* transform each of us. May you be next.

AFTERWORD

If you read this book again in the future, you may find it helpful to read through it in a different order next time. Below, find the chapters re-grouped according to whether they talk about your mental *limitations*, good *perspectives* to adopt, good *habits* to acquire, or useful *checklists* for you to follow.

LIMITATIONS

- 10,000 hours?
- Working memory

PERSPECTIVES

- Harnessing your mindset
- Stress: a primer
- Training "future you"
- Steering the supertanker

HABITS

- Clean pages don't count
- Do the steps
- Cut when you're sharp
- Repeated challenge
- Bite-sized chunks
- Improve the question
- Struggle with the early material
- Work like an expert

CHECKLISTS

- Verbatim memory
- Trust yourself, trust the process
- DARE: Devise, adjust, repeat, execute
- Be your own pilot

ACKNOWLEDGMENTS

To my students and their parents: you, "my families," have helped me to develop and to test these ideas by accepting my help, trusting my counsel, and granting me the great privilege of watching (and sometimes helping) you grow. Thank you for giving me the gift of serving you.

To my friends and colleagues in the Bay Area Tutoring Summit: Thank you for keeping me sharp and ever-vigilant for new ideas.

To those who read and improved early drafts of this book, including my wife Audrey Khuner (writer and editor *par excellence*!), my former business partner Justin Sigars, Dr. Ben Bernstein (my Chapter 9 guru), Chris Borland, Matt Cohn (my Chapter 7 guru), Scott Cowan, Ted Dorsey, Nathan Fox, Eliza Khuner, Eric Nehrlich, Morrisa Sherman, Phil Webster, and Devon Ysaguirre: thank you for sharing your wisdom, and for allowing me to pass it off as my own. You are true coaches and teachers.

To my long-time friend and colleague Dave Denman: thank you for your early faith in me, and for first (and often) suggesting that I write a book.

To my family: thank you for following your paths, and for trusting me and mine. Together we have created a strange and wonderful road for ourselves.

ABOUT THE AUTHOR

Wes Carroll is in his sixteenth year of tutoring and mentoring gifted students. This is Wes's first published book.

> www.wescarroll.com
> wes@wescarroll.com

Made in the USA
Las Vegas, NV
24 November 2020